CURIOSITY

✺

CURIOSITY

✽

PATRICK WHITFILL

NEW MICHIGAN PRESS
TUCSON, ARIZONA

NEW MICHIGAN PRESS
DEPT OF ENGLISH, P. O. BOX 210067
UNIVERSITY OF ARIZONA
TUCSON, AZ 85721-0067

<http://newmichiganpress.com>

Orders and queries to <nmp@thediagram.com>.

Copyright © 2020 by Patrick Whitfill.
All rights reserved.

ISBN 978-1-934832-72-1. FIRST PRINTING.

Design by Ander Monson.

Cover image: ID 78527677 © | Dreamstime.com

CONTENTS

Part I: Curiosity

Greetings from the Golden Record:
    I. French   1
    II. Akkadian   4
    III. Spanish   7
    IV. Hungarian   9

Part II: A Theory for Almost Anything: Electromagnetism
    (1)   12

Part III: Curiosity

Greetings from the Golden Record:
    V. Bengali   14
    VI. Dutch   17
    VII. Welsh   20

Part IV: A Theory for Almost Anything: Gravity
    (1)   23

Part V: Curiosity

Greetings from the Golden Record:
    VIII. Sinhalese   25
    IX. Zulu   28

Part VI: A Theory for Almost Anything: The Strong Force
    (1)   31

Part VIII: Curiosity

   x. Korean   33
   xi. Polish   36
   xii. Mandarin   39
   xiii. English   41

Part IX: A Theory for Almost Anything: The Weak Force
    (1)   43

Notes   47

Acknowledgments   49

In a nutshell, Mars needs you.
—Robert Zubrin

*I'm trying to mean what I
mean to mean something.*
—A. R. Ammons

As to my mother, she is obsessed with fire.
—William Carlos Williams

CURIOSITY (I)

Hello to everyone.
—French Greeting

The first joke goes: suppose I told you how
often I draw bangs on women that I haven't
met and who don't wear bangs? That I sketch
between us, or erase, depending, finger-length

strands of hair that rest below the eyebrows
and above the eyelashes? My index finger
gives me away, because I can't help but
scratch at the air, so that, on some atomic

level, I'm moving the universe around their
faces into bangs. Because I like to. My point:
the punch line remains the same, no matter
the question or the joke or the soundtrack.

The truth is: I want everyone to have bangs,
not only women. I want children and
squirrels, deep fish without light in their lives,
Space Aliens, toothbrushes, mongrels, cats,

presidents of sovereign nations, their
presidential pets, to all have bangs. And
telekinesis. I want everyone to be so identical
to everyone else that the term *everyone*

becomes redundant, like spitting into a lake
to see if you understand the concept of
volume, how it operates, how movement
determines opacity. A week ago, I woke up in

Minneapolis with a bucket of spring waiting
outside. Here's the punch line: because gray
doesn't paint itself. Here's the joke: why did
Minneapolis wake up with a bucket of spring

waiting for me outside? Everything is a set-up
everyone falls for at least once. Everything
consists of two parts: the way up and the way
back down. The morning I first woke up in

Minneapolis, I rolled over and wished that it
never happened, Minneapolis, I mean, maybe
the whole waking up experience, which never
meets the standards I place on prepositions.

Just once, I want to say *Minneapolis* in such
a specific way that it sounds like the start of
an aria. I want to know how to speak in aria,
how to sign in aria, how to fall apart, pick

myself back up and cry in aria. I want to know
aria for "I want," and never say it to anyone
else but myself. Let's pretend for a while
longer that space exists entirely on one

premise: that wishes happened once, eons
ago, and someone forgot to make one, which
was the only one which came true. I want to
say *Minneapolis* and mean angels exist. I want

to say *Minneapolis* and turn heads, break
fingers, shatter the previous record for
number of times people wept for no reason at
once. I want to say *Minneapolis* and not

regret a single sound I made in doing so. I
want to say *Minneapolis* and not regret
anything. Please understand that when I say, *I
want*, I mean, *I give up*. I mean, *it never

should have happened this way or any other way, so I
might as well wish against the whole thing.*
Say *everyone*, and mean Minneapolis kills
with a thousand different tongues,

all replete with aria. Say *everyone*, and mean you
once woke up and meant it. Say *everyone*,
and then stop speaking for the rest of the day,
of the year, of your life, and see if that feels

anywhere close to what it may feel like to
choke on space. To live in space. I want you
to know that, if I aria, I would only aria to
you, which by *you*, I mean you, Minneapolis.

CURIOSITY (II)

> *May all be very well.*
> —Akkadian Greeting

Pretend for a moment that afterlives exist.
Souls ascend, descend, appropriately,
according to whatever system makes the most
sense: good, up; bad, down. Good, here. Bad,

way out there. It doesn't matter. Pretend that
we could exorcise decency in this manner.
Last night, I watched for only the second time
The Pianist and thought the ghetto scene later

in the war, before the first rising up, where
the Nazi Colonel randomly yanks men out of
their work line to shoot them in the head,
pausing to reload his gun, did happen

historically. And if that did happen—and not
just then but any time in the sick lifeline
scarred into the palm of history—where some
man or woman purposefully obliterated life to

celebrate the wingspan of cruelty in its finest
throttle, I wonder what happens next,
epistemologically speaking, I guess, in that
murderer's life's schema. What I need before I

can agree on anything existing beyond just
the temporal and annoying is proof that
consequences exist that go beyond the body
universal. I need everyone at home to turn off

the movie, hold each other over the popcorn
bowl and bourbon and over the dishes
concentrating into themselves their dozen
distinct sets of ketchup-stained fingerprints.

Already, we've begun the process, surprisingly
tedious though it proves to be, of picking
Earth's first colonists on Mars. I would like to
propose that we can still hope that all of those

people who deserve an afterlife comprised
years away from anyone else who would like
nothing more than some cotton candy
popsicles and maybe another person to run

their fingers along the nape of his or her neck
while they watch a television show about
cupcakes, that those other people, the ones
who have killed with anything approaching

a suitably applicable definition of *glee*, the ones
who deserve what we might as well call *Hell*,
would have to colonize Mars, and never get
anywhere with it, never find the well-spring,

never make the air better, never stop radiation
from peeling the skin off of their eyelids, even
though they will have a certain topical cream
that comes in aerosol form that they have to

use every night, if Mars even has a night long
enough to do so, where they must spray their
eyelids back on, which takes hours and hours,
so they can close them just for a little while.

CURIOSITY (III)

Hello and greetings to everyone.
—Spanish Greeting

I can believe in Feynman, in physics, in
the neutrality of armadillos, of deer cast off
semis' grills on I-75, leaving Kentucky on
Memorial Day weekend, where, as a species,

we remember to slap a boat and Ski-Doo to
the back of an Explorer, hit up the lake,
the condo, the unforgettable motel we didn't
know doesn't allow lap dogs or smoking. I

can believe in the nebulous. How else can I
say this? In Kentucky, I lay next to you, and I
didn't finish a sentence, but I drank both of
our glasses of water. This is how I say *I love*

you in drunk. This is how I sing these days: on
an air mattress in the Bluegrass State, a
comforter from high school. In Kentucky, I
showered with a baseball cap on because I

wanted to remember the sensation of delaying
gratification. In Kentucky, an insect the size
of a wadded-up Kleenex smacked the wind-
shield and disappeared. I remembered Texas,

the highway from Plainview to Lubbock, how,
on my last day in town, a yellow-breasted
sparrow smacked hard on the windshield as if
she'd aimed for it. I always assumed every

yellow-breasted sparrow was a female and
a mother because I once shot a yellow-
breasted sparrow sitting in her nest, guarding
her nest. I shot her half a dozen times with

a Daisy, and she would not fall. This was in
the country. This was before anyone had
determined the exact position of the sun. This
was before anyone had told me about how

mothers operate on their young. In Kentucky,
I refused to fall in love on an air mattress. In
Texas, I killed a sparrow that could have been
a swallow and did not care to know if there

was a difference. In Kentucky, we didn't talk
about Mars, but I bought a book with a red
cover so that I felt like I was learning. Listen
to me, please: In Ohio, I drove a woman back

to her house and made love on an air
mattress. This is how we fall in love in this
century: by driving to and away, by not
knowing the color of the breast we've shot.

CURIOSITY (IV)

> *We are sending greetings in the Hungarian language*
> *to all peace-loving creatures on the Universe.*
> —Hungarian Greeting

Come jazz sax with me. Come peace at home
with me. I want the incidentals of your last
car-wreck, and if you didn't have one, I want
the lie you'll tell the insurance company my

heart employs. I want to talk about my heart
and mean space, mean Neptune, mean
Andromeda, mean gravity gave a shit once
and always more. Come bass line with me.

Come 90s rock with me. Come Electric Slide
with me. To all the peace-loving creatures of
the Universe, we got nothing. A whole bunch
of it. And pickles. A cultural delicacy, no

matter the working definition of *delicate*, of
which, culturally, we do not agree. Come
space with me. Come voyage with me. I'll
Peter Pan and you green-legging, you Wendy,

you second-star, and I'll straight-forward til
occultation completes itself, and where we
land, the dust of it in our ankles, we'll call that
Mars, the surface of a handmaiden goddess.

Come lose your shit with me. I've got all our
accoutrements in a basket, though my basket's
the size of two closed, befreckled man's
hands. I'm sure you understand. When I rang

yesterday, I told you about my tooth, how it
woke up to wake me up in the middle of my
night. This is what you do when separation
anxiety depends on an agreed-upon distance

apart. Come universal with me, come occult.
Come pretend you have a general interest in
the physics of the future, and I'll pretend I
invented my voice and used it only for you in

the hours before my morning runs. Truth is:
I want to love Hungary tonight, and make
them some grilled cheese sandwiches, tomato
soup, draw some blueprints up for a decent

escape path in case of another bad land war.
But not that, too. What I want is for
something to come across and say *Okay*,
because space makes sense, the way fireflies

don't and ropeswings do, the way physics will
if you let it dissipate enough. To be clear: I
do not care about Mars, though I know I
should, and I will not call my mother because

she's like Mars, in that, we all have a concept
of it we do not wish to reach out towards
fully. Someone should write more about
pigeons, about the noticeable exhaustion of

old guitar strings, about monster truck rallies
gone majestically right, about snow clowns,
shock tops, brutal disassociative devices
employed by someone who should write

about those initial thirty seconds when he
realizes that what I wanted will not come my
way, and then the following two minutes
when I realize what I wanted is available

and that I probably had it already: that
one good glove, a garden bit of basil, movie
tickets in a pocket, already torn in half, one
smelling like that French scent you loved.

A THEORY FOR ALMOST ANYTHING: ELECTROMAGNETISM

(1)

Because each story deserves somewhere safe to keep it, just in case, I'll tell you that this one never happened, not in the way that we've grown accustomed to the cause and effect of things, the way they link to one another, never not separated: but, out at Lake Mackenzie, back in high school, a group went out there, John David's folks had a trailer near the water's edge, which was too shallow to call it a dock, more of a tongue of wood that couldn't lick itself wet, and we went out there one summer night, near the 4th, and I thought how much money they must have to own land this close to water, and we went out there in our pick-up trucks and with our coolers, and I don't remember what lie I told my parents that night, what reason I gave to disappear where the canyons yoke up like shoulders around the wind coming straight down the plains from Canada with nothing but the geese to get in its way. And sure, I had already fallen into the kind of love with one of the girls out there that meant, one night, I'd confess it to her, out in a field on the tailgate of my truck, and she would tell me *No*, and ask to go back to the party, and we would, and the night at the trailer, I had taken on the sullenness of a drought-addled lake, trying to find a way to let people know they could float right across the face of me and all I'd do is remember them forever for it, but John David pulled out these Roman candles, bags and bags of them, let them pour out in front of the trailer, and yes, rain doesn't fall there enough to make of the lake a lake, and yes, we could have burned down miles of land because we had lighters and nothing else to do with ourselves but see what could catch on fire if we didn't run fast enough, and Lilly didn't run fast enough, and John David fired a candle at her, because we had started our Roman candle war, and Lilly didn't know that war with a bunch of farmers' kids meant either finding a place to hide—front room of the trailer, back of the truck, in the next county—or firing back, and so she assumed no one would actually launch at her, but near her, the way war should be fought, all warning shots and next times, and when John David aimed at her, or near her, because who can accurately predict the lifespan and trajectory of a firework bought on the side of a highway between Plainview and puberty, and it caught in Lilly's hair, in the tangles of her hair, and I think about how shiny her hair must've been then, full of the grease of her youth, the sheerness of her youth, and the ball of flame caught in it like the back of her head had spit out a fireball, and whatever product she used went up, and her hair went up with it, and she ran, arms flailing the way no one runs unless they're running away from their own selves, and jumped into the lake, and smoke rose around her in halos and steamed and steamed and stunk enough that John David had a joke for that, too, something about burning out the skunks, smoking them out of their dens, which is what you do with anything stuck in the ground: you burn it and you burn it and you watch it roll out in

       the hope water's somewhere and water's safe.

CURIOSITY (V)

Hello! Let there be peace everywhere.
—Bengali Greeting

In *Ghost*, Patrick Swayze defeats, among other
things, the Pauli Exclusion Principle, the law
of physics which posits an electronic
resistance between surfaces. Thus, you sit not

so much on the chair but on an impossible
hovering of just-above the chair. I know this
doesn't matter. None of this. Not even
the Pauli Exclusion Principle, though I do

appreciate what it does for me. Last night, we
made a *paella* and margaritas, and I spent
thirty minutes telling her about saffron,
how it's made, how they harvest it with their

hands, how it takes fields and fields, and when
I finished telling her what I knew, I read her
the Craig Arnold poem I'd been paraphrasing
the entire time. Place enough zucchini in

a dish and anything can feel like a salad. Pour
enough tequila in a blender and every night
can turn gorgeous in an overheated kitchen
no bigger than a space habitat. We bought

three bottles of red wine and did not drink
them. *We'll live longer tomorrow*, she said. Now
that becomes the issue ahead of me, to live
longer tomorrow every tomorrow. To

concentrate my emotions on a single object
and somehow convince my electrons to
magnetize and move. Look: I know
I can become vaporous, punched through

like a wall made of loose dirt. What made
Swayze Swayze was a controlled mullet, that
kind of quarter perm that does damage to
bangs, that does damage to the early 90s, that

destroys a just-thrown clay pot on the wheel
and makes everyone a little bit muddier. Dear
Clara Ma: I wonder if you'll ever watch *Ghost*,
if you'll ever escape Kansas, the sixth grade, if

you'll look up when the solar sails blow past
our orbit and wonder where your name went
into the universe. Dear Clara Ma: I want you
to know that everyone on our planet should

love you just a little bit, the way we love
a good song, a solid haircut, the smell of our
clean sheets in someone else's dryer. It takes
enough of these small loves to map the solar

system. Do you see this, Clara Ma? Do you
see how Kansas has become a kind of blood
vessel, irradiated by your right hand in the air
of your sixth-grade classroom? Do you see

how much you've changed the course of
interplanetary exploration? Give it a name
and you give it a purpose, Clara, and that purpose
will let the rest of us know how to fall

in love with it. Last night, I stepped outside
after we finished throwing our dishes
drunkenly together and did not put on my
shoes, and I did not step through the door

and did not sit in the white, plastic chair. I did
not see any passing cars or pay attention to
stars or to the rustlings of the possums in
the bushes. Oh, if I only had better hair, Clara

Ma, the way I stood there, only my feet to
touch the ground, I could have been Swayze. I
could've beaten the Pauli Exclusion Principle.
I guess I'm saying that I could've been dead.

CURIOSITY (VI)

Sincere greetings to everyone.
—Dutch Greeting

Here's where entropy begins to take over.
A random weekend, the bed of a Ford on
a turnrow somewhere between Nazareth
and Edmonson, and, yes, someone would

have rolled a blunt, but that wouldn't make
a difference to our conclusion, because, by
then, given the wide circumference of that
year's drought, the fact of a blunt provides, if

the phrase applies, a kind of alternate ending,
but that wouldn't matter, because this would
happen on some random weekend, and in
the back of that truck, Nathan would stand

up, though we're doing fifty, now, easy,
and DW puts his foot almost all the way
through the bottom of the accelerator, trying
to stand up straight, Flintstoning that fucker

until we hit a speed fast enough to prove to
ourselves that we don't care about what
condition we let our bodies die in, because
nobody looks too long before they give up,

blink it all away—so Nathan stands up, starts
yelling into whatever dust that has yet to rise
from the road, like he's calling to it, making it
trust him, and, sure, this doesn't make any

sense to me, but I need to laugh at it anyway,
to make it fake by laughing because,
otherwise, the pressure unsettles me, strips me
down to those precarious rocket-bits of bone,

thought, and blood. But then you'd have to go
forward to Mexico, to a night where Nathan
leaps off a balcony, flips in the air and did not
die, though he wanted to. This all comes

down to Lawson's Criteria, so you must have
your certain pressure, your certain heat, your
certain amount of time before fusion. I do not
know what happened to Nathan, where he

landed after he landed on a Mexican hotel
resort's porch, after he landed at a hospital,
after he landed on a gurney and then at an
airport in Texas, after he landed in

Portland for a few years, after he landed in
Jack Daniels and fell in love with a bad person,
but I do know what it means to fall apart near
a language I do not speak. I do understand

the difference between a scream and a plea for
mercy, and the difference is one of feeling
compelled to finish it. Here's what I think
happened: it would have been a weekend,

and the truck would have gone all the way to
Hale Center, and we would have stood up in
the bed and yelled, and nobody would have
understood that the fusion we had, with

the pressure of Texas in our faces, turned us
both into flashing rockets passing out of
town. What I'm trying to say is, given enough
pressure, anything can turn into a bomb.

CURIOSITY (VII)

> *Good health to you now and forever.*
> —Welsh Greeting

Occasionally, I discover how all the leaf ends
littering the yard have gathered to form
a single event in the timeline of the street,
a new entity, if, by *entity*, I mean any

gathering of anonymous parts into something
that assimilates into a whole, the way colonies
of ants can do, each one about as smart as
a thumbtack but, linked in their slips, smarter,

gathering cat food from a crevice behind
the washer, dismantling a mountain of a sweet
potato on the oven, they change, same way
snowdrifts start separate, then layer

themselves, then gather to become a snowball
or snowdrift; so it goes too with leaves
and leaf ends in the gutter, clustered in such
a way it's nearly impossible not to think of

the word *nest* when I step over them and stare
down, mesmerized less with the combination
of twig and leaf than I am, if only for a bit,
with their ability to turn a plurality into

a singularity and not lose anything from that
conversion but, in fact, one could argue, gain
an entirely new event which incorporates
them both. It's like that between us, I think.

Just last night, you woke me up without
meaning to when you said, in your clear alto,
the word *space*, and then fell back to the dream
you must have enjoyed enough to share with

me. And as with the twig and leaf and gutter, I
tried to consider the implications of that
syllable, of all the syllables tangled in your
throat, and that you would say, of all of them,

the one that I have not stopped talking about
these past few months, and wondered, while
the cat mewed around my arms and the rain
outside slanted, drizzling a little more than it

would later this morning, if, by *love*, we don't
mean this moment, when one states in a clear
voice what the other one can't stop thinking
about—but that only works when the other

wakes up a smidge at just the right time to
hear it, and had I not, had I continued
dreaming about whatever useless unraveling
slipstream I had dreamt up until then, then

would that not also become a kind of
definition on the conditional hilarity of love?
I'm kind of like that today, partly a cluster of
twigs and leaf ends situated in the curb

outside my house and partly the boyfriend
who woke up at the right time to hear you
summarize my fascinations over the past year
into a single sound. And, as it would have

taken me not waking up at not the right time
for that to have no meaning, so could
someone, or something—a squirrel in a hurry
to avoid the tabby, maybe—could unsettle

the twigs and leaves so that, when I stepped
over them this morning after pulling
the trashcan to the curb because it's Tuesday
again, I wouldn't find anything noticeable

about them, which, I suppose is another way
of saying that I have an interest in singularity.
But it makes no sense, I would argue, that,
after I recognized the possibility of a nest, I

felt an urge to unsettle them, to kick a couple
twigs, because, even though I appreciate its
existence, I seem to appreciate my presence
within its existence, my disturbance, more.

A THEORY FOR ALMOST ANYTHING: GRAVITY

(1)

What I want to talk about today is fire, but the sun's out, and a few minutes ago the daughter of a woman I knew back in high school went to the hospital because the cut she gave herself on the inside of her thigh went deeper than she expected, or maybe it cut exactly as she expected, but either way, the cut spilled her into a waiting room. Back home, wildfires spread like mayonnaise across the horizon, a smearing whiteness everyone knows the taste of, everyone clicks their tongue against their mouth's roof of just to get the palette to release itself, let the breath back down. Because everything's down. Even though it's winter, here, I manage to find myself sweating in bed, and, today, I trust how clouds stay in one place long enough I have to wonder what they think about shadow play, if they even care, because I trust not only that my body sweats but how it does so, meaning in specific areas, with just a hint of brine, as if you finally cut deep enough you'd find that I'm all olives, all martini, all dry skin patched with light. I'd like to say to the girl who took apart her flesh like some manageable mistake looked back on, two particular lies about how the body works in relation to the self: 1) that bodies work in relation to self, and 2) that this means something, but nothing seems to matter that much when the blood wells, meaning it comes from the bottom up, meaning that what makes the body warm defies gravity because the heart's a muscle that works so hard we have to call what it does a rhythmic beating. But here's the thing I know about gravity: gravity's just another attempt to impress us to ourselves, which has the kind of pillowcase in its logic I find myself putting my hands against just to make sure I can feel a flimsy thing all the way into its fibers and still not believe it makes any difference whatsoever. And if you take all of that together and push it down into small enough passages so they look like veins, and laid them out in a straight line, you could say this girl with the cuts finds herself like a kind of fire the head can't put out, and doesn't even want to, and she's got these scars running down her thighs, but the horizon's flat enough for long enough that the only things she's worried about being let down by sound like gravel pushed down hard enough it can become something new, a road, asphalt, a black and tarry diamond, because that's the other thing they say about pressure and gravity and fire and the blood your body is:

    beaten down is how we're built to feel for far too long.

CURIOSITY (VIII)

May you live long.
—Sinhalese Greeting

Let there be more Mars in your diet, more dry
tea bags, cosmic dust. Let there be horse carts
Phaeton forgot to hobble stashed near
Cassiopeia, near Jupiter's micro-solar system.

Let there be more gods: god of toothpicking,
god of summer dresses risen against the thigh,
god of humidity. Let your inner Egypt
trammel you with Cessna-dropped leaflets

ranting against the way lotion calcifies near
the lid. Let your inner Egypt possess many
nameless mutts scampering away from
Martian debris, destined for international

acclaim. Let your inner Little Curly not melt
upon take-off but find its way back to some
back street in Moscow, back to training, back
to just another Laika-licensed quadruped who,

against great odds and odd politics, goes on
living forever. Let your inner Egypt and your
inner Little Curly meet up one evening on
your inner dance floor—all hard polish and

mahogany counters—and let your inner DJ
play all the right records, only couples' songs,
roller-rinking the two through the salted
business of Motown, and let them fall in

a desperate, shuttle-deployed kind of love. Let
your inner parachute fold so many times
together you defy physics. After too many
grappos, may your inner social barometer

malfunction. May you marry indiscriminately
and always in a rush. May you handle poorly
some nuance no one informed you of
beforehand, and may you laugh it off. Please

understand that praying in the new century
vacuums your inner Egypt and, once done,
discovers your inner Atlantis, and may God
bless your inner Atlantis. Let there be another

afternoon so close in temperament and degree
to your favorite one, your Tahitian evening.
May you stand tall in a shower not your own
and declare the soap unrighteous, because

your stink is holy and so is theirs, because
today feels like the kind of day where body
odor came from the gods. God of the armpit,
god of the noon showering. God of morning

breath. Let your inner Egypt declare you holy
without sacrifice, though sacrificial lambs will
be found, catalogued, and released near
rye fields. Let your inner Laika mate

with your inner Nakhla, and may you bark
long, without a lozenge, without a shuttle. Let
there be another day in your pipeline. Let
there be someone waiting for you at home

who also enjoys women's golf and talk radio,
who also pretends to sleep when you pretend
to sleep, who also wakes up early because
coffee wins over the hope of another

dream. Let all of this be true, but more than
that, let the flies surrounding your porch fall
for you one night, and let you remember
that the gods these days are mighty small, that they

have a billion eyes all pointed at you, that they
have wings and grow from maggot sex, that
they do not mind what you've done because,
to them, it's all a bit confusing anyway, with

your two feet, your thumbs, your inability to
land on shit and find sustenance. Let your
inner Egypt catch one and hold it until its
buzz quits, and may you let that god live long.

CURIOSITY (IX)

We greet you, great ones. We wish you longevity.
—Zulu Greeting

Today we've had rain, had it with rain, the *it*
some essentiality each possesses in minute
portions, just as today becomes linked back to
today's corndross, today's crowshank, today's

stationary, *et. al.* We all slip through that way,
interweaving grooves, smooth sometimes,
sometimes more of a trained beagle breaking
apart at the bark. I've read again today

another three sections of a long poem and
played against it, the poem, the Bill Evans
and Chet Baker LP I bought after I bought
the record player, and Side A plays how Side

A plays, all the grooves finding the needle
fine, but Side B, maybe because of finite
follicles of cat hair, or the wear and wax of
unchecked dust flecks, creates a steady static

in the background, but also not exactly *in*
the background, but part of the foreground,
on top of the music, yet the static sounds too
much like a sax, a tenor sax, with a separate,

more beboppy melody, as if, in the other
room of the studio, Charlie Parker played
"Salt Peanuts" into the adjoining wall, and no
one told him to stop. What I want in order of

its possibility of coming true: 1) to sound
much smarter than I am; 2) to play piano
the way Evans did, in that one octave finding
more notes than the keys create, but

not earning that right to play that way, not
wasting away the way he did, not with his
cocaine and the drinking, but with the thick-
rimmed glasses, the bent over the keys frame,

the in general sunned approach to losing it.
Today we've had rain, which breaks hearts,
but what if today contains a groove
replaceable with a beboppy copy of

the original, and it's somehow much greater,
shoved against the wall of this perceivable
day, slamming against sound-proof doors
so that, on occasion, we cock our heads, tilt

an ear to the clouds, double-check ourselves,
only to continue throughout the afternoon,
going to the grocery store for a recipe
involving lintels—which you've no idea how

to handle—and waiting in line with our
phones out to thumb across a text we've not
known we've been waiting for all day. But
there it is again, a quick three-note riff up

the chromatic scale, a run the fingers make,
and you can catch the tail end, the way you
can see a squirrel change branches only
because the preceding branch still sways.

Because if that's true, then that means we
have another track laid down, and we only
have to pay attention to that possibility—that
separate *it*—to change, as a second, ascending

note will change the melody into a kind of
harmony. But, yes, I'm also aware of how
pointless all of this is, I promise, and I can
recognize that static remains static, that

Parker didn't play in the adjoining room no
more than someone else has a lifeline played
against the one I have today, the 4th of July,
where it doesn't rain all day, where I still want

someone to bring me a sparkler, where I light
it in the dark of the living room and nothing
happens, but I imagine that it does, and I
draw my name in the smoke the dark allows.

A THEORY FOR ALMOST ANYTHING: THE STRONG FORCE

(1)

Nobody smokes anymore. Used to, I'd go outside first thing after waking up, light a cigarette, and, for at least a few minutes, note each breath leaving like they mattered, like they took up space, had mass, made some kind of difference even if only in the air. Now, nobody smokes. But still, whenever it gets cold enough to watch the way heat escapes us, meaning in blooms, if we're being ridiculous about it all, and we are, aren't we, most of the time, being ridiculous, wondering out loud about what else to call the shape of the thing disappearing from our mouths, as if we had anything to say anyway, and what I'll do now, instead of smoking, is stand there on the porch, so nobody can see me, and I'll breathe. Somewhere in Texas, my mother smokes another of what she calls her lady-thin cigarettes, ashes right on her loveseat, and does not budge when the phone rings. Look, the last time I bought a pack of cigarettes, I stayed up all night to finish them because I believe in the value of punishment, that I have to make up for most of everything my body has done by using my body to do it. In this way, I feel like I fall in love, and this is how I understand love, not that everything goes back to it, but wouldn't that be a kind of smile we could tuck into the heart like a card from a person we'd like to meet. None of this matters, the way we connect, the ways we don't. Let's say you've never smoked, never took a little too long in the stall in high school to see what would happen if you lit up there, the pack

in your underwear all day because as much as you needed
to buck the system you also needed to hide it from actually
happening. In the back of the house, where we keep the extra
things we figure everyone needs, but just not now—afghans
from dead grandmothers' living rooms, throw pillows, mouse
traps—I have planted at the bottom of an empty flower pot
a pack of menthols and some strike-anywhere matches, and
even though I'm not necessarily waiting for the phone call that
tells me exactly how my mother died, I keep my phone in my
pocket anyway, checking it like the face of a plant I don't believe
the bloom of, and when it comes, which it will, regardless,
just know that I'll break into that pack, that I'll strike each
match until the flame flares up the dark, and when I breathe in
cigarette after cigarette, no clean breaths between, I'll do it as a
kind of eulogy, as proof that the body can

                        die a thousand times before it starts on fire.

CURIOSITY (X)

How are you?
—Korean Greeting

Somewhere down the fog, a road broadens,
becomes a lake, becomes a lake house.
Somewhere down the road, I meet this girl
whose hair begins like a myth the Vatican

suppresses, but poorly, and she doesn't wear
lotion or socks, and she doesn't mind the way
I fall in love with other people's books. If we
meet, I'll find a way to teach her about bow

shock and occultations, and when we run out
of candles, I'll have her say *Candles* to me until
the lake breaks into thin ice and steams
the windows. I'll say *Candles* back to her, go

outside, have conversations on a deck. I wish
I had more decks. What I know for sure: that
the chances of finding the Golden Record are
infinitesimally significant, that, if the Record

showed up in the backyard of your average
American citizen's house, they wouldn't get
the graphs to make the stylus work.
Somewhere, the person who you first fell in

love with has decided against eating dairy for
a year, and, for some reason, the choice
happened because they no longer wanted to
be reminded of you. This is how messages

work: we send them out so that the people
around us will know that we sent them out.
Somewhere down the lake, a body floats up
the side of a log and stays there. Somewhere

down the body, a fish has nibbled. But this
isn't a dead body, it's just a body, the way
space isn't a problem anymore, but an
approachable sigh. Listen: I said *Candles* this

morning because I want to start a new chant
in my life, want to have that purpose, that
control, that view on the angle of the day. I
said *Candles* this morning because I can't

imagine anyone disturbing graves without
using a flashlight. (I would like to disturb your
grave but I don't want you dead.) Somewhere
down the fog, another fog beckons, folds in

on itself and becomes a cloud. This is how
change occurs: without a point of reference.
Somewhere down the road, another road.
Somewhere down the road, a bench with

extra nails and a *Do Not Sit* sign falls into dirt.
I'm trying to place myself and call that
a *Candle*, a unit of measurement the way
the hand measures the horse, the foot the line.

I want to talk about *Candles* as the unit of
degree for how much you care. I'm about
twenty *Candles* into her. I'm all *Candled* out.
I'm all *Candled* out. You see? We sent it out

because we didn't know how to send it to
everyone, the messages, the ones that said,
*Okay, okay. We got your Candle. We love your
Candle. We all have the same Candle.*

Somewhere down the *Candle*, the lake
explodes. Somewhere down the *Candle*,
the bass become rainbows the way oil
becomes paint. The way fog becomes an oak

becomes a forest fire. Somewhere down
the road, in the lake house, the pillows won't
get any softer than they are now. I'd say that's
about four *Candles* short of a *Light*. And you

want as many *Lights* as you can get, because,
in the end, that's what you pay out with, that's
what they want at the gate. Otherwise it's all
stumble and fall. It's all stub and trip you up.

CURIOSITY (XI)

Welcome, beings from beyond the world.
—Polish Greeting

In the movie version of my life, we resurrect
Jones Very, and then ask him to explain why
some angels hide in stripmall displays, see
what sweetfaced Ole Holy Ghost has to say

about that. Jones Very, I have a surprise for
you: the Holy Ghost moved to Philly around
1975, met a wonderful young man at a flea
market and they've bred corgis ever since.

People love them. Mint dresses their table like
ribbon-spreads. Also, the Holy Ghost took
a vow of hypogramania and won't shut
the fuck up near its church. In the movie

version of my life, I have a delicate interest in
the curvature of my hair, and I lick my lips
like this: up up down down up. In the movie
version of space, space gets played by Jones

Very, his two-year psycho trip into the mouth
of the Holy Ghost catalogued by train
whistles and a girl humming through her
blues. Dear Jones, Dear Very: Someone

comes knocking at the river's door and no
one pretty answers. Imagine this, Jones Very:
every satellite we've sent into space has not
actually met space, only Low Earth Orbit.

Voyager hits the heliopause with a shuffle
step, rolls on for another infinitude and does
not sing about it the way you would have,
Jones Very, your jaw bearded with sweat

and honey, your hands already flying into
swans that the river wanted for keeps. Dear
Jones: we don't have men like you anymore,
and when we do, we do our best to burn

down their houses and piss out the ash-swells
with flares. Look: if we wanted to hear what
the Holy Ghost had to say, we would've made
it so that our satellites come back without

having to use the words *crash* or *failure*, *burnt* or
outmoded. Dear Jones, Dear Very: I would like
to fall in love with the vertiginous destruction
of forestry, with the sound of a napping foal.

Dear Jones: how important is it to you that
we've landed on Mars? In the movie version
of that happening, you refuse to hear
anymore, trudge off into the just-now-falling

snow near Merrimack, and refuse to hail a cab
or call a friend, your trench coat tight around
you like another, more decent spine. When I
come to look for you, the scene turns out too

hard to film, and so we have to sit off-stage,
running lines, coughing into our hands to
keep them warm, because snow isn't allowed
to simply fall around us, and this snow isn't

a prop, and the cold frosting from clouds
actually exists. And when I thump my chest to
keep it warm, you smile, because I'm doing
that heartbeat thing, that song you recognize.

CURIOSITY (XII)

> *How's everyone? We all very much wish to meet
> you, if you're free please come and visit.*
> —Mandarin Greeting

I cling too often to some self-effacing mirage
of myself in nature—say some black cat
mangles some squirrel, or when
the neighborhood possum deposits its nest in

the bush whose name I'll never learn rears up
at night its two dinted, reddish eyes and does
its best witch impression—and attempt from
that to determine my next best available

move. I believe in Mars because I have never
seen it, because it can create for itself
a separate descent into pronouncing our
universe. I believe in space because, at heart, I

have a terrible fear of it, of immensity, of
possibility, which is why I encourage form
and boundaries, why I respect laws and follow
the rules. Does this make sense to you?

I occupy such an insignificant snippet of this
it's an insult, like pissing on the altars of the
gods when they still showed up to gather the
apples from the storeroom, when they still

commissioned hymns, when they still sent
their sons and daughters down here in fishnet
stockings, when they still made love to us
and stole from us our last few words before

we had to move on to other cities, to other
families. That's what I'm doing: I'm trying to
bring back, not the gods, really, but those who
would bring to them sacrifices to their woods.

CURIOSITY (XIII)

Hello from the children of planet Earth.
—English Greeting

Over a year ago, I lived in a cabin with
a deer's head screwed into the west wall,
the setting wall, and read, one night,
the introduction to Plato's *Republic*, and had,

as I've had before, and recently, the distinct
realization, a sensation similar to an iceball
with a pebble in the middle of it smacking my
chest, that I have nothing to offer. Listen to

me, please: this morning, sitting at my desk, I
wept a little, but hard, into my cat's fur, who
had jumped up on my lap once I started
hitching, and I was someone brushed off

a crow with a splintering toothpick, gathered
up dust particles, and I'm just a sign on them
that says, *Patrick*. Dear Jones: you should get to
know Clara Ma someday. Dear Guerrero:

most days, I have to slap myself to make sure
that I remember the thirteen-year old version
of myself that would beg a mirror not to look
like that, not to have that face, not to stare

that way, to look that way, and I slap myself
because I forget how much I've gone away
from that, and I can't put that on a Golden
Record, and I can't explain that to someone

by referencing Plato—not that you can't or
that someone can't, but that *I* can't—but I'll
do it again tomorrow. But the strange part
isn't that I'll slap myself in the morning to

remember what I used to beg myself for, but
that, after a few months go by, when I forget
to slap myself and then, one day, for whatever
reason—a wren hits a fence post, falls; the cat

misjudges the couch, slips off—I'll spend an
afternoon taking turns with my open palms
across my face, crying some, crying more than
I should. How do you put that on a record?

Dear Mars: I'm not going to see you, not in
person, not even in the night sky, because I
don't know you. I don't recognize you. And,
honestly, Mars, I never really cared about you.

A THEORY FOR ALMOST ANYTHING: THE WEAK FORCE

(1)

Non-contact force. In this, we can sit in two different states of undress and still manage to affect the other. No one looks outside, and this will not become two cardinals, no matter how mad they are at being cardinals, at telephone wires and the false sense of communication they still so desperately imply. This will not become a love poem, but in one state of undress or another, we have in our skin a faint okayness between us, and this should become for us a way to consider the necessity of that. Imagine this: in my office, I have both of my hands up, the stop gesture, and I keep them this way for ten minutes out of every hour, and as I have them this way, you stay in the other room, and in another state of undress, and this is not going to become an ode to distance, but anything that breathes has in it the innate power to keep away the air that makes up the self. Some days, I fall apart and spend most of my time in the truck, putting on and taking off again my seatbelt, refusing to start the engine. In this, you feel implicated, can hear the non-contact force of a non-started engine, which is significantly louder than a started engine when you're expecting to hear a started engine. In one state of undress, you and I have a family together, a daughter, maybe a son, maybe at some point both, and in that moment, we have taken apart the ribs between us and made from them a slide, a tabletop, a finished and folded fitted sheet. One of us the tucked corner, the other one tucking it in. Tonight, before we fall asleep, we'll spend a few minutes not talking about non-contact force with anything but the tips of our fingers, which evolution has designated as the most permanent expression of our separation, of our distinction from the other, from any other, and so with our family, and so with any family, and if we were to spend the rest of the night maneuvering from room to room, all the lights turned off, just the two of us, in various states of undress, moving from room to room with the tips of our fingers letting us know when it's a doorjamb, when a window, when an almost dead basil plant, and when we have had time enough to let our eyes adjust to the dark, and we can see outside, all of the magnolias all the way until the mountains somewhere north of here spreading over the street like night is just a suggestion that the rest of the things that breathe don't have to take us as seriously as we tend to take us, and what little light we havebetween us will let us see the other's face, will let us tell the nose from where the mouth opens, the way the sky sometimes does, and the space above that, too, and even though we won't need to touch the other, though we never need it in exactly that way, when we could see us without the need of our hands, we'd still let our fingertips graze the corners of lips, the flutter in the ribcage, the breath leaving already and not having anything or anywhere else to go, lingering in between our fingers until it settles in a palm and rests there,

        knowing it has no other decent place to go.

NOTES

The Curiosity Rover launched on November 6, 2011. It landed on Mars on August 6, 2012. Its goal was to determine if Mars could have ever supported microbial life.

Moore's Law—attributed to Intel's co-founder, Gordon E. Moore—states that computing power will approximately double every two years. This will eventually run into the issue of atomic and quantum computing, as the rate of progress is directly related to the ability to make smaller and smaller microchips.

The Theory of Everything attempts to combine the four elemental forces in nature: electromagnetism, the strong force, the weak force, and gravity.

Panspermia posits the idea that life on Earth began from microorganisms present in outer space first.

Little Curly and Laika were dogs sent into space.

Gonzalo Guerrero was a sailor from Spain who shipwrecked off of the Yucatan peninsula. He was put into slavery, eventually earned his freedom, and stayed with the Mayan people, raising a family.

Jones Very was a contemporary of Emerson, a poet, essayist, and mystic who would eventually be put into an insane asylum for his beliefs in the Second Coming.

Clara Ma was a Kansas student who is credited for naming the Mars Rover, Curiosity.

ACKNOWLEDGMENTS

Some of these poems have appeared with different titles and/or in slightly different forms. Thanks to the editors of *Boston Review, Wreck Park, Kenyon Review Online, The Adroit Journal, The Equalizer,* and *Southern Humanities Review.*

PATRICK WHITFILL has work appearing in journals such as *Boston Review, The Threepenny Review, Kenyon Review Online,* and *Southern Humanities Review,* among many other journals. He's lived in South Carolina since 2008, and he teaches at Wofford College, where he co-hosts the Wofford Writers Series. He lives with two dogs, a cat, a wife, and a son named Jule Jasper.

>

COLOPHON

Text is set in a digital version of Jenson, designed by Robert Slimbach in 1996, and based on the work of punchcutter, printer, and publisher Nicolas Jenson. The titles here are in Futura.

❊

NEW MICHIGAN PRESS, based in Tucson, Arizona, prints poetry and prose chapbooks, especially work that transcends traditional genre. Together with DIAGRAM, NMP sponsors a yearly chapbook competition.

DIAGRAM, a journal of text, art, and schematic, is published bimonthly at THEDIAGRAM.COM. Periodic print anthologies are available from the New Michigan Press at NEWMICHIGANPRESS.COM.

www.ingramcontent.com/pod-product-compliance
Lightning Source LLC
Chambersburg PA
CBHW031502040426
42444CB00007B/1179